Se

MW01643768

by Helen Stanley
illustrated by Gerardo Suzan

HOUGHTON MIFFLIN HARCOURT
School Publishers

Copyright © by Houghton Mifflin Harcourt Publishing Company

All rights reserved. No part of this work may be reproduced or transmitted in any form or by any means, electronic or mechanical, including photocopying or recording, or by any information storage and retrieval system, without the prior written permission of the copyright owner unless such copying is expressly permitted by federal copyright law. Requests for permission to make copies of any part of the work should be addressed to Houghton Mifflin Harcourt School Publishers, Attn: Permissions, 6277 Sea Harbor Drive, Orlando, Florida 32887-6777.

Printed in China

ISBN-13: 978-0-547-02832-3
ISBN-10: 0-547-02832-6

4 5 6 7 8 0940 18 17 16 15 14 13 12 11 10

If you have received these materials as examination copies free of charge, Houghton Mifflin Harcourt School Publishers retains title to the materials and they may not be resold. Resale of examination copies is strictly prohibited.

Possession of this publication in print format does not entitle users to convert this publication, or any portion of it, into electronic format.

Winter, spring, summer, and fall.
These parts of the year are
called seasons.
In Farah's town, each season
has different weather.
As you read, look closely to see
the seasons' changes.

Winter is cold in Farah's town.
Snow covers the ground.
Farah brings gloves
when she plays outside.
What do you think
Farah is building?

In Farah's town, spring is mild.
It's not too hot and not too cold.
Leaves and flowers are around.
What does the wind carry high
in the sky?

Farah's town is hot
during the summer.
People wear light clothes.
How is Farah keeping cool?

Fall is cool in Farah's town.
The leaves turn bright colors
before they drop.
What is Farah doing?

Do you know why every season in Farah's town has different weather?

It's because Earth tilts, or tips to one side, as it circles the Sun.

This picture shows Earth in each season.

Look closely.
The part of Earth where Farah lives is tilting toward the Sun. That means there is spring and summer.

Look closely.
The part of Earth where Farah lives is tilting away from the Sun.
That means there is fall and winter.

Farah visits her grandma in the winter.
The Earth doesn't tilt as much where her grandma lives.
So the weather there doesn't change as much. It is warm in the winter!
What are your seasons like?

Responding

TARGET SKILL **Main Ideas and Details** What seasons does Farah see each year? Make a word web.

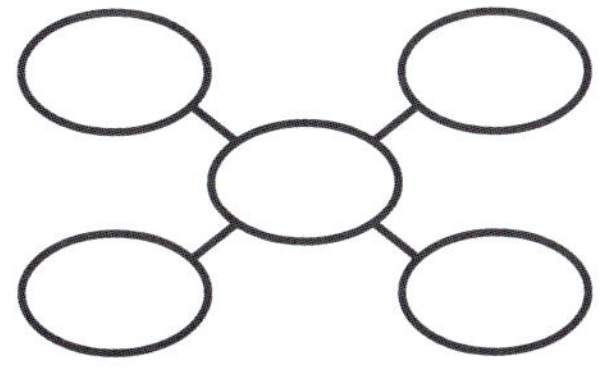

Talk About It

Text to Text Think of another book that talks about seasons. What seasons are in that book?

around	carry
because	light
before	show
bring	think

TARGET SKILL **Main Ideas and Details** Tell important ideas and details about a topic.

TARGET STRATEGY **Question** Ask questions about what you are reading.

GENRE **Informational text** gives facts about a topic.